LADY SUN & LADY MOON

POEMS BY DIANE STEIN

LADY SUN &
LADY MOON

POEMS BY DIANE STEIN

THE CROSSING PRESS
FREEDOM, CALIFORNIA 95019

Acknowledgments

Some of these poems appeared in: *A Letter Among Friends; Daughter Visions; Focus; Full Circle; Goddess Rising; Greater Golden Hill Poetry Express; Harvest; Island Lesbians; Kalliope; Maidenspirit; North Country Anvil; Of A Like Mind; On the Rag; The Original Coming Out Stories; Rubyfruit Readher; Sisters United; So's Your Old Lady; Telewoman; The Wild Iris; The Wisewoman; Womanspirit; Women's Network; The Women's Spirituality Book; Pagana.*

Library of Congree Cataloging-in-Publication Data

Stein, Diane, 1948-
    Lady sun & lady moon : poems/by Diane Stein
        p.   cm.
    ISBN 0-89594-495-2. -- ISBN 0-89594-494-4 (pbk)
    1. Women--Poetry. I. Title: Lady sun and lady moon.
PS3569.T3635L34 1992
811' .54--dc20   91-35758
                                                        CIP

For Sue

CONTENTS

Chapter I Lady Sun & Lady Moon

Queen of Hearts 15

Lady Sun & Lady Moon 16

Moth Touch Woman 17

Occult 18

Carbon 19

Orbits 20

Looking 21

Lattices 22

Eclipse 23

The White Cat Moon 24

Shadow Casting 25

Beltane 26

Daughter Poem 27

Mermaids 28

Alignments 29

Kliegs 30

Torch 31

Minerva Disrobing 32

Psyche 33

Daphne, Sky & Grounding 34

Camouflage: Daphne 2   35

The Lady With The Unicorn III 36

The Lady With The Unicorn IV 38

1 The Lady 39

2 The Unicorn 40

3 The Pair 41

Pomegranate 42

CONTENTS

Chapter II Eve Her Story

She & I 45

Squash 46

Breasts 48

Blood 50

Gym Clothes 51

Slapped 52

She 53

Anna's Gold 54

The Woman Who Could Write 56

Spice 58

Tau 59

Kissing 2 60

Birds 61

Spooning 62

You didn't Say 63

November Eve 64

Shopping Bag Poem 65

The Strike At Saint-Nizier Church 66

Southern Dykes 68

Interlacing 69

Eve 70

Listen I Have Found You 72

Introduction

My first writing was poetry, though I am known for my books on Women's Spirituality and healing. From the age of fifteen (1963) until beginning *The Kwan Yin Book of Changes* at thirty-five (1983), my writing was primarily poems. Poetry taught me how to use words, how to put them together in precise ways for clear meanings. I began publishing poems in 1969, in the small literary magazines of the early women's movement. These were publications with shoestring budgets and circulations of usually under 200, that collectively became the backbone of the lesbian feminist movement of the 1970s and early 1980s. Most of these magazines were the work of individual women. The women's literary network was the mainstay of my life for many years. Many of these magazines no longer exist. They are a part of women's herstory that deserve remembering.

The poems of this collection go as far back as 1976 and as far forward in my life as 1988. There is only one poem written after 1984 and most were written in 1982. They were influenced by the developing feminist and lesbian feminist movements of the 1970s, and the beginning Women's Spirituality movement of the late 1970s and early 1980s.

Though I had over 400 publication credits for single poems before *Kwan Yin* and though I submitted manuscripts frequently, no book of my poetry was ever published. It is a dream of thirty years come true to publish this collection now. Writing poetry about women's issues, lesbian issues, and lesbian love was a radical act in the 1970s and '80s, and in the conservative America of today it becomes a radical act again. Perhaps we need a little more of the militancy of those earlier times and a little more pride in women's heritage and who we are. Many of these poems to women are also poems to the Goddess. Those that appear here have stood the test of time. I offer them to you with joy and woman love.

I believe that women are Goddess and can do anything.
I believe in living one day at a time and taking the
    future in easy bits.
I believe in women and I love them.
I believe in my work, that the writing and teaching
    channeled through me will help to make a better
    world.
I believe that life is abundant and has good to offer
    everyone.
I believe we can survive the pain and heal ourselves
    and the earth.

I
LADY SUN
&
LADY MOON

Queen of Hearts

lady you hold all the cards
and play them close
to your perfect breasts
you are Priestess and Empress
of the World
Strength to my Fool
i dream us on the Wheel
of Fortunes turning
as the Towers fall
as the Lovers
Stars
and Sunshines
dance a liberated Moon

Lady Sun
&
Lady Moon

you align with sun
who are my lady moon
your torch ignites
my shadows
priestess
of cooler flame
your flares spark
sharp as lasers
and you ash
my softer glow
your cycles glare
with gold
and glitter
char my phases
scorch my silver hands
your furied
solar seasons
burn my constant
shining nights

Moth Touch Woman

"the Goddess blesses us in fire"

—Starhawk

creature of fire
sun diamond
touch that draws
to burn
glitters and chars
as i flutter
close to you
helpless
i cannot move
my hand away
cannot turn my eyes
from your light
from your brightness
from your heat
this melting
and this flimsy ash
oh sparkling one
oh lioness
oh flame

Occult

your fleetest thought
will draw me to you
there will be no miles
i come with petals
springtime
in my hands
my black hair free
i come to you
with love

lady you must never
be afraid
we are who we are
we cannot
shut each other out
if you call me
i will come to you
always i will come
i am waiting

i am waiting for your call

Carbon

the year ends
and years begin
tunnel of diamond
tunnel of coal
circles charred
and one still
flaming
your eyes lead me
round the burning
jewels of hopelessness
you beckon me
then hesitate
we almost spark
almost ignite
this time
our karmas reach
and sputter out
again again

Orbits

you spin
a life of your own
faster and faster
and i spin mine
more slowly
beside you
untouching
wishing for you
as we turn in line
two planets
of one galaxy
or planet
and a moon
we spin
our own elipses
our own orbits
speeding separately
in turn
in paths as strangers
swung together
never reaching
we move only
side by side

Looking

looking
into clear streams
you see me
the moon
you see yourself
constellation
woman of stars
gazing
at water
midsummer
bright darkness
you stare
into sky
seeking reflections
the heavens
still faces
you recognize
two

Lattices

light
that weaves our
startled eyes
your eyes to mine
moon reflecting
on a universe
a net of stars
this goddess web
this magick
of the pair of us
of who we are
conjuncted astrals
comets
two and twin
a matrix spun
in orbits reaching
bright with love

Eclipse

the engagement of your arc
your eyes catching mine
igniting kindling flaming
more than light forged new
heat engulfing spark
engulfing torch
engulfing fire
your fire eclipsing mine
my fire eclipsing yours
scalding melting merging
burning flickers
two as one
steady conflagrations
melding
hot embracing
our penumbra as we flare

The White
Cat Moon

the white cat moon
looks out
with diamond eyes
she sheaths her
silver paws
her candle tail
streams
brightness
as she switches
hunts
her beaming
whitewire whiskers
choose
her next best phase
the white cat moon
licks
platinum on
her sparks of
gleaming fur
the white cat moon
is satisfied
she stretches
lights
and shines

Shadow Casting

she is the woman in the moon
bright oceans to my salt thirst

her fingers silvered radiance
flow down my mind in sleep

she is there alive in night streak
in the luminence of dream

my lady of the crystal moon
she takes my lips again

shadows of her brilliance
blend our breasts and shining hair

her eyes my eyes warm candle scent
glow reachings softly two as one

waking dies ignites our colors
disperses us to deserts

glaring burns to drying glister
she is gone and scorched with sun

Beltane

celestial
you are stars
you are night skies
bright above me
shining free
with silver hair
you are the path
the light of beltane
constellations
every planet
gleam of taurus
you glow mysteries
all we share

Daughter Poem

my daughter stares at me
from the clouds
moon in taurus
almost beltane
and she wants to come
wants to come to me
i watch her shining
and i reach for her
my golden star
the lady of the silver moon
looks down at us
and smiles
i reach for her
she reaches out
my daughter smiles

Mermaids

she dreams into eyes
that halt
and surf cannot betray
the very sea life stills
i raise my hands
to her hands
and silver mirrors raise
she is salty she is warm
she is mother she is child
we stare into each other's eyes
we are oceans we are sibyls
we are women giving birth
she glistens
and she shimmers
i am emptied
drained of colors
as she splashes
swims away

Alignments

afraid
you turned away
two planets in conjunction
we have met our stars
forces of all universe
have pulled us close
have brought us
face to face
to see each other's eyes
and whats beyond
inside
two stars/two moons
two planets
joined in passing
locked in reachings
destined and unclaimed
afraid afraid
of this in all of us
you turned away

Kliegs

when the floods
drip topazes
through your hair
rains of glowing light
and strands of it
drizzling golden
pouring candlebeams
streaming jewels on you
you stand there
brighter than the gems
the brilliant drops
of orange-red flames
and you sing cool
in raining arcs
of crystaled gold
of jewels
they enflare you
embrace you
envelop aura
and transform you
they soak molten
and they prism you
your dazzled hair
your melting eyes
they saturate
they shine and flow
with love (my love)
they sparkle glitter
loving you
my love

Torch

the crack of a struck match
or slapped face
startled redness leaping
scorching glow into curled paper
dream by dream
consuming
brittle browning
blackened ash

you will not look at me
past light
past warmth
you will not recognize
or speak
i hold my hand to you
and heat is in the air
you spark and twist away

hearts dont burn
they say
my own goes up in flames
i watch it in your fireplace
where you are cool and gone
i watch it in your fireplace
it burns it burns
it burns

Minerva Disrobing

(A painting by Lavinia Fontana)

war comes home tired
armor bloody
sword too long to lift
she carries her large metallic
helmet in her hardened hands
her hair is stiff with dust
her eyes are burnt with grit
she drops pieces of her
outerwear spread harsh
around the room
the owl and olive tree
look on and watch her stretch
her body is a womans
in a womans perfumed bath
she washes off the sweat
the death the scent
of severed limbs
the pain and gore
she wraps herself in pastel
velvet towels
war dresses in a négligé
of polyester pink
she bends to do the housework
first before she sleeps

Psyche

Psyche searched
she sorted all seeds
for her seed
and all darknesses
for her light
she sought for her daughter
in death and awakening
sleep and consciousness
she sorted galaxies
and dust
Psyche searched
for her in sterility
and she searched for her
in birth
pregnant Psyche
searched and Chaos
silent watched
she suffered
and she smiled for her
she smiled for Bliss

Note: Psyche and Chaos
were eventually reunited.
Their daughter was Bliss.

Daphne
Sky & Grounding

straighten straighten
feel the plunging into dark
feel the pull of earth
and bound of center
plunging deeply
dropping fully
grasping grip and holding
become root
become descending
become connecting and entwining
with the source of strength
running power
of the ground

straighten straighten
sweeping higher into sky
feel the wind and rain
through branches
lift through starlight moonlight
leafing budding fruiting
and returning sky to earth
bending rise of light crown
become planet
become soil
circle sources rising
rising falling
to the ground

Camouflage:
Daphne 2

i have frightened
startled you
to your roots
your lifting arms
branch back from me
small birds flee
your leafing
clenching hands
your eyes of sky
shift closed
and look away
you huddle
shuddered
as for storm
your colors darken
skin toughens
body stiffens
at my touch
you bow and turn
and rise above me
and lean colder
into rain

The Lady With
The Unicorn III

(the lady sees)

"Oh unicorn,
the world will make a myth of you and me
the world will always disbelieve us."

—Robin Morgan

None knows us for ourselves:
my maiden left us, fled:
she'll one day meet you
too — or if not you some
woman who must be to her
what you become to me.
other pairs of twins exist,
as you and I.

Oh Unicorn, I had no birth as Lady
till you touched my hand.
and you were not the magickal,
the mystical, until
our eyes transformed
this each of us to one —
to you and I.

Oh Unicorn, oh Lady,
we are both one beast.
no real explains such
union of two females here.
in myth we'll goddess be:
like centaur male and stallion,
like sphinx the sage and lioness,
we two are one.

None knows us for ourselves:
they wont believe, refuse to, fear.
they'll redesign you masculine,
bright spirit that you are;
they'll redesign and call me Mary,
not the Lady, though I am not she.
our daughter will return with swords.
we two are one.

The Lady With
The Unicorn IV

(they speak as one)

"that I might behold
what you beheld
beholding this,
my one desire."
                    —Robin Morgan

1
The Lady

this mystery
my one desire.
you stare at me
awaiting.
not opposed
but longing
in your wonder.
tentative. afraid.
the knowledge
of us both
is in your
golden eye.
the silver
of our touch
to touch
is in your
skin.
we stay
stare
within
our moment.
its the
moment
of our lives.

2
The Unicorn

this mystery
your one desire.
inevitable.
unfailing.
though still
unfulfilled.
our instant
poised.
my glowing
eye
your reaching
hand
will meet.
no turning
backward
only in this
going on.
ahead.
the transformation
of our selves
begins —
with no way
out
but through.

3
The Pair

this mystery
our one desire.
what we
sought for
always.
barely knowing
what we
sought
until this
finding
of our eyes.
blue eye
golden
melting to a
single sight.
reachings
of our skins
become
one skin.
pairing
of our bodies.
minds.
become
one soul.

Pomegranate

love apple
moon blood
womans flesh and tears
tears that stain the hands
tears that fill the heart
the womb with fruit
seeds that stain and bleed
persephone ate four tear drops
from inside the ruby world
tasted blood from beneath
the poppy flower
beneath the clitoris crown
she ate pomegranate
woman seeds
chose flesh and blood and tears
chose mortality the spiral
gained summer/winter/spring
gained giving living birth
chose to change sweet stasis
for the sweeter tasting wheel
for monthly blood
for sensuality
for womans seed and fruit
gained blood
gained milk
gained salt and honey
and she tasted/gained the dark

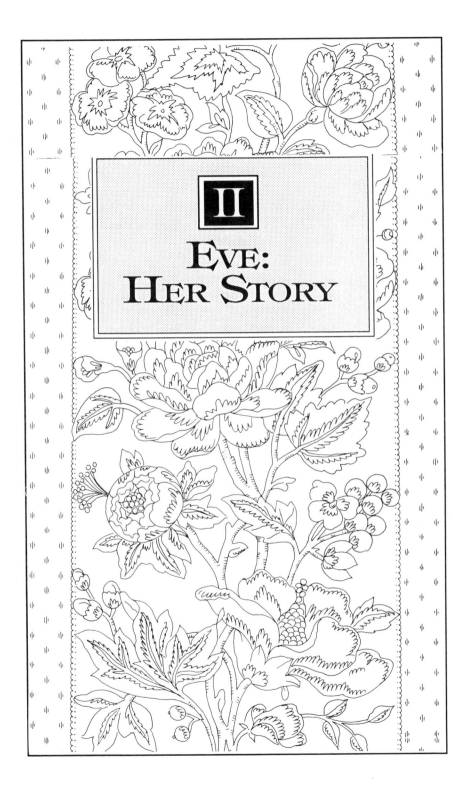

II
EVE:
HER STORY

She & I

when she & i were 6
we chased each other
round & round an open lot.
declared ourselves wild
thoroughbreds no man could catch

no matter how he tried.

when she & i were 9
our 4th grade teacher
called on 1 of us in class
& always got us both.
we answered to

each others names.

when she & i were 12
she said I couldnt walk her home.
she said she had another girlfriend
& she didnt want to talk.
she said that she was growing up.

& didnt need me anymore.

when she & i were 14
& were strangers
still I hadnt understood....

Squash

when I was 6
the first grade class
sold garden seeds 10¢ a pack.
door to door I took the envelopes
with wonder-sounding names:
marigolds and poppies,
portulacas, beans and gourds.
no one wanted to buy gourds,
or beets or squash,
when nothing else was left.
my mother gave me
dimes at dinnertime and threw
those seeds away. laughing when I
screamed at her, she sent me off to bed.
"Are you going to eat a squash?"
she asked, but didnt tell
me what it was.

Before I fell asleep
that night, surrounded by
the animals and dolls, I told my
stuffed-toy children of the flowers
I could plant. every seed
from every packet
would grow tall and green.

I would pull up every dandelion,
and chase away the neighbor's
kid who ran his tricycle
down my rows.
one day when I came
to water them everything
would bloom.

nasturtiums
would be orange and red
all on one stalk. sweet peas
purple on the fences,
pink cosmos
and pansies yellow on the ground.
I would even have white roses,
though there were none
in the box. my teacher
would be proud. then
I would pick the string beans,
watermelons, corn on the cob, gourds.
And even eat the squash. my
mother would be proud, too.
everyone would have
to love me then, with gardens
of my own.

Breasts

i didnt want breasts
they were dangerous to have
something for men to laugh at
father & his friends
something for mother to yell about
youre growing up to be a woman
cant play baseball anymore
something for salesclerks to sneer at
your preteen elastic first bra
(isnt she a little young yet
we dont carry them that small)

& in 7th grade
you didnt dare wear undershirts
& didnt dare go bare-chested either
inside blouses they would know
7th grade girls would know
& if you didnt have breasts
you wore the white straps anyway
filled the cups with kleenexes
that never stayed in place
pushed your front way out
& made believe

but since i didnt want breasts
& tried to hide them wearing
teeshirts sweatshirts pullovers
& tied a belt in there too tight
they said i wasnt being cool
7th grade girls wouldnt talk to me
7th grade boys called me flatty
father said i needed a good lay
& mother said wait a few years & see
while i slouched around with my head down
so ashamed i avoided them all

Blood

she said that once IT happened
id grow tits/grow tall/grow hair/grow up
be woman not a girl/
she didnt tell me what IT was.

i saw my mother in the bathroom
push the door shut tight
and yell for me to go away/
i saw the wad of cotton in elastic

and i saw the blood/
the messy blotting on the plush/
red tears on her thighs
running down.

she said that once IT happened
IT would happen every month/
id have to ask for Kotex by myself
embarrassed in the store/the druggists smile.

and worst of all she said
that once IT happened for the first time
i could have a child/
and be a total shame to her

but didnt tell me how.
she told me when at last IT stopped
and didnt happen anymore/
id be so old as good for only dead.

Gym
Clothes

regular id say
every swim day
regular
it was a code
we whispered
a code the
teachers used
it meant
menstruation
periods
the curse
i hadnt
started yet
didnt start
till i was
almost sixteen
i was afraid
of the pool
the teacher
glared at me
counting Rs
in her gradebook
change into
your gymsuit then
she said
and wait

Slapped

(for my mother)

i learned not to cry
slapped once
slapped twice
i stood still
turned away my face
and let her slap again
again
defiant daughter
of a mother
who couldnt cope
who couldnt control
who grew red
at slapping me
as me she
battered everyday
i didn't let her
see me cry
see me bend
i walked silent from
her punishments
and cried alone

She

she is a small and quiet woman
with a fire in her gut
the kind that no one
notices till she explodes
or suicides
and then they wonder why.

her hair is neither
brown nor blonde
her eyes not
green or gray
they meet her in a moment
and as soon forget her face.

but she is gay
and she is bitter
she is proud
and she is free
she is poetry and music
and the moth that roared and flamed.

she is the voice the cry in all
of us our fear our light our pain
the brightness that will scald her
to her death will spark our wake:
we will not have the sense
to love her

no one else will take her place.

Anna's Gold

(for my grandmother Anna Backman
on her 72nd birthday)

When she was nine,
her mother took the rings
from Anna's ears.
In America, she said,
you'll have a better pair,
or two pairs,
where the streets are
paved in gold.

Anna left Roumania
believing all she'd heard.

New York
was never walked on wealthy
coins or even brass.
Fortunes never fell from trees.
Pennies came from piecework
and from doing things without.
They didn't buy bright jewelry
but the simple bread.

The holes in Anna's earlobes
since her birth grew closed.

After she'd been married,
moved to Pittsburgh
and had raised two girls,
Anna bought
her golden hoops.
With potato and a needle
she repierced her ears.
Her daughters

and her granddaughters
knew prophecies in gold.

The Woman Who Could Write

(for Ingrid B.)

you know how it is —
you spend 8 hours a day
running a goddamn
xerox machine to live
on 80 bucks a week

an hour at lunch
in wishing
for release (on rye)
dont try to read
theyll poke you out their door

and 2 more hours
on subways
getting pinched
by grinning
men

walk in to making dinners
scrubbing toilets
settling dogs & kids disputes
drop in bed exhausted
(with the tv) before 10 pm

when is there time to write?

you're 'the girl'
at work surviving
just a robot maybe worse
at home a part-time mother
or the maid that cleans & cooks

alone
(when you can get it)
you're a poet
with a strong
& conscious mind

thats when nothings
start to happen
nothings written
nothings finished
nothings tight enough to send

and you're judged
a threat existing to
each master in your life
till you're silenced
(& you're fired)

you're a woman who could write.

Spice

you are cardamon
cinnamon
rosemary thyme
i put leaf of you
in shoe to see
you walking
through my dreams
you are sage
and wise
your hand leans out
in lavender
to flower night
you sweeten tea
you are apple blossom
spearmint
parsley greens
at noon
you add rosehips
sandalwood
to morning
you are chamomile
orange peel
ginseng root
and chives
i plant you
in my garden
in my senses
in my life
you are herb of all
bright summers
you are spices
you are spice

Tau

i reach
through holes of blackness
voids of space
through airless
soundless worlds
of vacuum crowds
i reach for you
through twists and arms
of frozen galaxies
of planets/stars
to find you there
somewhere
that orbits coming home
i reach for you
for gravity
for color/breath
your ocean eyes
your windy hair
i reach through emptiness
for earth and light
i reach for you
for only you
i reach
i reach

Kissing 2

i was you
coming to love me
you ran into my arms
as if no time
no lives had gone
between
you remembered
and you knew
we knew
i wore blue and gold
to beckon
and we watched us
watched
until the you was me
and i was
someone shining
bright at last
as part of you

Birds

men have always tried to fly
built rockets and wings
imitations
women have always been birds
we lie here together
two women
smooth feathered
hearts beating
and we take each other
high into flight
your wheelings my swoopings
we tumble
singing aeronautic migrations
hot rufflings
our lovings our freedoms
as nestled we soar
and we rise

Spooning

we fit together like silver
spoons in a velvet box
nest on quilted nest
your gleaming head
lies shining on my shoulder
my glowing body beveled
polished in your arms
we are warm as mothers soup
we hardly weigh each other down
we sleep the sleep
of stainless innocence
our handles carved in rose
we sleep the sleep of recognition
rested living metals
who were cut of one fine ore
we hold each other
in our formings
bodies same to same
we love and sleep and stir again
until you wake me
and you lay me tarnished
and without you
in a dark grained wooden drawer

You Didnt Say

you didnt tell me
when you left
you wouldnt
be back
the nights would be
all night
& in the morning
youd be gone

November Eve

we see each
from the other side
a film of water in a cup
our crystal ball
day staggers and
the night preys long
the moon swells full
and dies
i see you love you
reach for you

the ending of the year
this ending of our year
the turning of our lives
autumn oak leaves
pomegranate
pinecone apple
mother of dried corn
i light warm candles
to remember
to remember
do you remember me
at all

Shopping Bag Poem

(for Rochelle)

a line on any subject
two lines
ten
poem for a meal
sonnet for
a place to sleep
or being instead
hungry
wet in doorways
on what restaurants
throw out
roaming
with the dogpacks
and the winos
in the cities
at the curb
nothing for her own
shopping bag woman
when her lines
dont sell
and heiress
when they do
she juggles
and she trades
and writes
just to survive

The Strike
At Saint-Nizier Church

(Lyon, France, June 3, 1975)

Gaining from Lyon to Montpellier
Grenoble Marseilles Cannes and Toulouse
June 3rd 1975 in all of France:
the whores have invaded the Church.

We have declared ourselves
members of the human race at last.
We have declared ourselves
women with the right to live.
We have taken sanctuary at the altars
of your spitting middle class
from laws that fine us jail us
and that keep us in the streets.
We have joined this strike to tell you
that from here we're going to fight.

We are no longer prostitutes
but sisters with a cause.

Cathedral priests were speechless.
And the cops were at a loss.
The Ministry of Women took a holiday to Spain.
The government pretended there was no one there.
Strikers came to Gods House
with their sleeping bags and songs
and bringing fruit and hotplates
and their grievance to be named.
They made the news and talk shows
and they entered every home,
reached feminists and housewives
and the governors and johns.
They reached them over Paris over
London over Brussels and New York.

For the first time we've been organized
the last time we've been stopped.

Southern Dykes 1984

i cant be seen with you
you're too out
too blatant
and i need my job
last year the university
got rid of a woman
when they found out
she was a dyke
oh they didnt put it
in those words in public
but we all knew what it was
when they couldnt
make her quit
they fired her

(what did you do?)
i kept my mouth shut
i watched
i helped them do it
i found a man to date

you northerners
are all idealists
dont tell me about the '50s
dont tell me that we have to fight
dont tell me about gay pride
or civil rights or sisterhood
or talk about community
or sticking together
honey this is the south
the closet
we do it to survive

Interlacing

electric web
that binds with spark
sends wire
sends contact
veins
enmeshed among
our eyes
between conducted lines
this life
our past lives
blue web
that jolts us close
shocks us
and transforms us
on each others
dreams
feeds each others
currents
blood
transmits each others
burning
needs
this web of red
of light and heat
of love

Eve

why are you shaking?
women shall come
from women's bodies
everyday,
but you of all
these women shall
be woman first.

lie there my daughter
and begin your breath.
i will lie beside you
and will whisper
things you do not
understand,
not yet.

but later you shall know them
not remembering
from where,
and men shall fear
as witches what we
women see as wise.

lie there my daughter
just a moment more.
women lie in women's arms,
and everyday
this shall be so,
though you are
still the first.

you shall not think
of being last
in womens hunger
or in womens love
when men afraid
of this shall try to
bind your hands and breasts.

lie there my daughter
there is much to say.
i must offer you
to man-type for awhile,
he who shall so hurt you
when you try to heal his pain.

you shall lift him
from your body
as i raise you now from mine.

Listen
I Have Found You

listen. i'm finding more of us
they've hidden/we've hidden us
too many years
we're here. we live we'll claim
our piece of earth

sisters
i'm so glad you're here
so glad at last to find you/know you
see the doubled womens
symbols on your fingers
breasts

listen
i can hear you see you
i can take your hand/our hands
and recognize
your eyes in mine
we are the same

sisters

there are things in us the same
there are things in you/in me
so different that are joy to share.
pain to share. and anger
and are love

listen
i have found you
and i hear you/see you
and we bring each other hope
sisters. i have found you
i won't lose you

we won't lose each other now

THE CROSSING PRESS
publishes many books
of interest to women.
For a free catalog,
please call toll-free
800/777-1048